**Missouri Center
for the Book**

જ્ર જ્ર જ્ર

Missouri Authors
Collection

Seed Time, Harvest Time

This book of poetry has been made possible by a gift
given in honor of

Gela Sessler

and the generosity and support of
Northeast Missouri State University

Seed Time, Harvest Time

Jim Thomas
Professor of English
Northeast Missouri State University

THE THOMAS JEFFERSON UNIVERSITY PRESS
AT NORTHEAST MISSOURI STATE UNIVERSITY
1990

©The Thomas Jefferson University Press
1990
NMSU LB 115   Kirksville, Missouri 63501 USA

Library of Congress Cataloging-in-Publication Data

Thomas, Jim, 1930—
    Seed Time, Harvest Time / Jim Thomas
      p.   cm.

ISBN 0-943549-10-8
    1. Adair County (Mo.)--Poetry. I. Title
PS3570.H5644S4   1990
811'.54--dc20   90-33637 CIP

Composed and typeset by The Thomas Jefferson University Press at Northeast Missouri State University. Text is set in Goudy Old Style 12/15. Printed by Edwards Bros., Inc., Ann Arbor, Michigan

The paper used in this publication meets the minimum requirements of the American National Standard for Permanence of Paper for Printed Library Materials Z39.48, 1984.

TABLE OF CONTENTS

Acknowledgments

Seed Time, Harvest Time, my first volume of poetry, has debts extending in several directions. Many of these poems got their first close reading from my students. Also, my colleagues have afforded helpful suggestions and provided valuable insights.

I am especially indebted to Jim Barnes for direction in assembling my manuscript and to Connie Jones and Joe Benevento for close readings. While over the years many typists have given me help, Miss Wendy Proffit and Miss Penny Ogren have taken great pains in their shaping of this book.

Grateful mention is here made of the encouragement of former and present administrators: Darrell Krueger and Jack Magruder, deans of instruction, and President Charles McClain and President Robert Dager have contributed a great deal. So, too, have Cal Huenneman and Ed Carpenter, my former and present division heads.

Without the invaluable suggestions of Professor Robert Schnucker, editor, and the work of Ms. Paula Presley, his assistant editor, this book would never have been completed, let alone been brought forth so resplendently. To Ray Jagger I am in debt for his fine photographs and his patience and understanding.

And last, I owe a great deal to my family who put up with me all these long years. My mother introduced me to poetry when I was a child; my father gave me a model of a good man. My children have grown and moved on into their good lives for which I'm pleased. Rita, my wife, has made me rejoice to be alive. To all of you, and especially to Rita, I dedicate this book.

Permission to reprint the following poems is gratefully acknowledged:

From *Kansas Quarterly*: "The Use of Concrete," vol. 9 no. 1 (Winter 1977), copyright Apr. 1977; "Poem as Waterline," vol. 12 no. 1 (Winter 1980 copyright Mar. 1980; "Bedtime Story," vol. 15 no. 2 (Spring 1983), copyright Dec. 1983; "On Grace," vol. 18 no. 1-2 (Winter/Spring 1986) copyright Jan. 1987; "Night Work," vol. 19 no. 1-2 (Winter/Spring 1987), copyright Dec. 1987; "Fall Murrain" and "The Honey Man," vol. 20 no. 1-2 (Winter/Spring 1988) copyright Dec. 1988; "Morning Windsong," "Enduring a Fall Rain," and "Salt in the Beer," which have publication and copyright pending. Reprinted with permission.

From *English Journal*: "Beast," (Dec. 1982); "Haycrop," (March 1985; "Escape," (April 1983); "Blue Entropy," copyright by the National Council of Teachers of English. Reprinted with permission.

From *Sucarnochee Review*: (Spring 1984): "Toad at Rest." Reprinted with permission.

From *The Old Red Kimono*, vol. 18 (Spring 1989): "Local Holy Man." Reprinted with permission.

From *Green Hills Literary Lantern* (Spring 1990): "An Aesthetic." Reprinted with permission.

From *Spoon River Quarterly*, vol. 5 no. 2 (Spring 1980): "Spring Hawks." Reprinted with permission.

From *New Laurel Review*, vol. 11 no. 1-2 (Spring/Fall 1981): "Moonlight." Reprinted with permission.

From *The Cape Rock*: "Great Jays" vol. 19 no. 2 (1984); and "View from a Lot" vol. 16 no. 2 (1984). Reprinted with permission.

From *The Fiddlehead*: "Lines for a Good Horse," and "Washing in Air," no. 150 (Winter 1986). Reprinted with permission.

From *New Mexico Humanities Review*: "Family Quarrel," vol. 1 no 2; "Windbreak," vol. 4 no. 2; "Open House," vol. 3 no. 1 (Spring 1980); "Morning Coffee," vol. 7 no. 1; "Three Evenings and Three Apples," vol. 9 no. 1 (Spring 1986); "Hunter," vol. 9 no. 3 (Fall 1986). Reprinted with permission.

From *Sou'Wester*: "A Breath of Cloves," vol. 12 no. 3 (Winter 1985); "Stout as an Oak," vol. 14 no. 2 (Fall/Winter 1986-87). Reprinted with permission.

From *Ball State University Forum*: "Dove Hunting," vol. 27 no. 4 (Fall 1986); "Desert Oasis," vol. 28 no. 4 (Fall 1987). Reprinted with permission.

From *Pacific Review* no. 2 (1983): "Mounds." Reprinted with permission.

From *The Midwest Quarterly* vol. 27 no. 2 (Winter 1986), "Cissy's Ciseaux." Reprinted with permission

From *Descant*: "Caress," vol. 11 no. 1 (Fall 1966), and "On Watches," (publication pending). Reprinted with permission.

From *Cimarron Review* 72 (July 1985), "Square Yard." Reprinted with the permission of the Board of Regents for Oaklahoma State University, holders of copyright.

From *Arete* vol. 4 no. 1 (Fall 1986), "Winter Sports." Reprinted with permission.

From *The Chariton Review*: "The Quilt," first appeared in vol. 1 no. 1 "Timber Stand," first appeard in vol. 2 no. 2. Reprinted with permission.

From *The Illinois Quarterly*, vol. 44 no. 2 (Winter 1982), "Smitty's Bar, La Plata, Mo." Reprinted with permission.

From *New Jersey Poetry Review* "Problem in Translation," vol. 1 no. 1 (Fall 1981); "Problem in Translation" and "Crawls" (publication pending). Reprinted with permission.

From *Paintbrush*: vol. 13 no. 25-26 (Fall/Spring 1986) "Loner" and "Thirteen Wheels." Reprinted with permission.

"Falcon with Kingbird" appeard in *Jeopardy*, vol. 24 (Spring 1988).

Some Hunts

On Grace

An awkward slow-moving clod,
I could not smoothly draw my knobby
fiberglass bow, twisty-grained, tough
as hedge. The string blushed
my arm raw; my breath wheezed raggedly;
my muscles shivered and jerked.
The wind stirred the oak leaves
and I did not see.
One day when the sun streamed
through falling maple leaves,
a doe turned brown statue.
Instantly the arrow snuggled
its string to my cheek,
darted across shadow dapple,
quivered in the grass beneath her neck.
The nearby creek sang on, the sun
poured gold on shivering leaves:
everything melted; I was the deer,
sun, trees. Something waved,
I bounded, I poured and flowed.

An Aesthetic

It is his own voice when it surprises him most:" "One Voice."
James Dickey

"It is only with the heart that one sees truly, never with the eyes."
St. Exupery, *The Little Prince*, trans. Giro Tomisaki

Just willin' hard right
words don't get 'em. "Look,"
they tell me, "use your eyes . . . "
Hell, I've skinned 'em
so many times now
I've got to get glasses.
"Then think what you see *means*,"
they say, dead serious,
when chances are not one
knows the green-spring spraying
splatter-plop of a cow . . .
Hellfire, they don't know
the nose-cutting stink
of a gut-shot rabbit
nor that fried squirrel
bones turn red! That's fact.
Most've never seen a red-tail
take a bird, nor a raccoon
dunk a dog. And *they* say, "Look."—
Well, I say just look
in there at them pictures
and *write* 'em, okay?
And keep it *simple*, hear?

Three-dollar Bill

Miss Young taught grades one and two
in the southwest, first-floor room
of the square, red-bricked grade school
in Louisburg, Kansas. All that remained
of the old high school north across
the street was brick veneer
on Mel Powell's house. He laid it himself.

For fifteen minutes before school let out,
Miss Young read to us. We'd straighten
up our desks (stuff whatever into
the dark space beneath the slanted top),
place our heads on folded arms,
and sink into the charmed circle
of her story-filled voice.

Once when I wasn't mesmerized,
I imagined what it would be like
to rise up quietly
and stand upon my desk.
What would they look like, my peers
hunched over their arms and desks,
all caught up in story or dream?

Above the book, her eyes staring into mine
rounded with incredulity. For a second
she paused, speechless. Then she cried,
"What are you doing up there? Get down!"
Following her gaze, their petal faces
turned as if they were heliotropic,
I the sun. I dusted erasers all week.

Spring Hawks

Courting, they sport high over our valley,
careless for once of all beneath them,
curvetting and dancing in the morning air.
They dare each other with loops and dives,
peeling off at the last split second
to safely touch, rolling, falling away
to flare up again in triumphant flight.
We watch them out of sight behind far trees
then splash through the mud to our car, the drive
over rutted roads to school and work, some part
of us forever gone on loan to hawks.

Timber Stand

I

Oaks' bare tops fill with bright gray:
dusky statue, I wait with my bow for deer.
Darkness seeping up from wet leaves laps
my hands; my white hat off
blurs against black oak.
I freeze against my trunk
as a squirrel crashes past,
leaps overhead to a nest.
I look hard at bare limbs
filled with nothing.

II

By lapping waves, gray teeth
on a small lake where
I've never been, the wind bites
my cheeks. A bay five bedrooms wide
separates me from a point
of oaks surrounding a picnic table.
The huge cottonwood behind me spreads
great limbs out over the lake
and almost above me; its vine
reminds me of a ferris wheel;
I look closer: a snake, huge,
its head almost over me, staring eyes.
Its tongue forks delicately out and back
testing my loneliness.
I look at my empty hands,
then back to the tree.
The snake's tail dangles quietly
with the slightest cat curve.

Leaping out into the waves, I splash across;
near the far shore, I stand up
thigh-deep. My hands seize
a stick angling up, weighted
there by a serrated crescent
of steel; I raise it, sprinkling
water in arcs to each side
of genuflecting waves.
The snake still hangs above the tree.
I splash to shore, teeming now with robed people,
eyes streaming in twisted faces
as they turn away. I walk through them
to a comfortable tree; they pass
deliberately to each side,
couple by couple vanishing.

III

I flex my bow, pluck a note from taut string,
and go into the woods by the lake.
Owls question the distance;
there is no singing
in this dark wood
unless you count the sighing oak
branches filled with nothing
moving slowly against bright gray
while the grove seeps
slowly full of dark.

Crawls

Bronze sentry lights flicker
off of thunderstorm pools
in the high school parking lot.
Half dozing, lulled
by radio's dreaming strains,
I wait a yellow bus
bearing the team and my son.

The lot isn't quite level; drained
areas are islands
floating in jet.

Something moves, a wrinkle
of light in the water.
I disbelieve it, sure
my tired eyes have tricked me.
A few seconds later it moves
again. Maybe it's a moth caught
by the storm. Distant lightning
glows; our old disturbance
sweeps into Iowa. Perhaps
whatever it is is drying
out its wings. I watch
a silvery wake of something,
finally rouse myself and stride
over to look. It stretches
its flimsy pink
wavering length, blind
tip quivering, surges
a quarter-inch forward:
an earthworm, a night-crawler.
Going back to the car, I step
carefully, seeing now
their many long tendernesses.

I smoke, watch the bronze
lamp silver their contorted
passages. Low on the horizon
the storm flares, my cigarette burns,
an unseen jet rumbles for midnight
Chicago. The earth-
worms move.

Mounds

"Rien ne resemble a un creux comme une bouffissure."

Sainte-Beuve

I

One rainy day we got back too late
for another call. We cleaned shop gear
and talked, mostly about hunting arrowheads.
Andy carried a bird point he'd found
near Yarrow. "There's a mound there," he said,
"I could show you. Walked all over that ground
as a kid. Hunting, looking for mushrooms
and, after rains, often finding flints. Hand-
axes — I've got three. Remind me — I'll bring
'em to work someday." We were talking near
a heavy table piled with tools — Turner showed
me how to make plenums on that bench. I'd
quit to go back to school; he'd stayed until
he decided there was no use and put
a gun in his mouth. When I found out, all
the flowers had faded. My plumb bob is
his — he gave it to me on our first job.
Every time I see its bronze arrow
shape, I grit my teeth and see him beating steel.
Andy and I looked out at the rain, gray
sheets veiling the alley; "Hope it ends soon,"
he said, "course, rain's good for the rhubarb."

II

My driver and I had endured our jeep
over most of the post's roads. We'd passed
a sign on the river road — an arrow
pointing off down a narrow trail toward
the Mississippi — dozens of times. The last

field day after our inspections he said,
"Do we have to go straight back to post?" I shook
my head. "Then let's look at those mounds." We
turned
at the dusty sign, wound down the bumps and weeds
and came to a turn-around. From the graves
shrouded by thick oaks, overrun by alders
and hazels, the river beckoned us: a bend
filled with sun glints, ruffled currents, and space.
Ambushed by the blazing light and quiet,
unforgiving mosquitoes, we listened
to crows rattling above the birches, looked
again at the silent mounds, drove away.

III

Having no car, she and I often walked
home in the warm spring from a movie, game,
or whatever we'd attended. Many
fine evenings we turned into the dark gate
of a nearby cemetery and strolled along
sharp gravel under high cedars and pines
to the little mound guarded by a green
cannon facing south, its wheels anchored fast
in concrete, its oaken spokes spongy and gray.
A tall spruce kept off the starlight; we talked
and sometimes sat or lay in soft bluegrass.
More than once we watched the moon sink behind
far treeline; the wind through dark needles breathed
faint black songs — even the grass whispered some-
thing.
A spring ran cold from under that hill;
my parents warned me away from it.
Thirsty, I drank from other, darker springs.

The Marking Point

As I sit inside the steel ribs
of my purring Greyhound, pausing
here in the heat and bustle of this Wichita
shopping center, a blonde carries brown
sacks, sets them into her car. Staring
furiously, she stands facing the bus;
the sun halos her — her dark eyes squint
at the glaring bus, she strains toward it:
her breasts, her taut hips, her dangling arms
say, "Take me with you . . . take me . . . "
She doesn't see me, know me, it isn't me . . .
magic car, simply to leave, to ride
thrumming miles away hidden
inside the green-glazed gray ribs.
Our driver's bored metal voice invokes Tulsa.
I watch her burning, feel her feverish eyes.
Suddenly thirsty, I long for her; the bus eases
out, picks its way through lights, busy
lanes of cars, emerges on a ribbon,
wide and sun-drenched, cutting the south wind.
Over the fields fly doves, gray hurtling forms,
compass legs tracing flight, courting.

Morning Windsong

Starlings rise out of the fall-touched oaks
and maples in a great feverish rush
of wings and rustling leaves. Against the clear
dawn sky the flock swirls and swings in and out
among the aisles of painted trees. The dark
mass seems doubly alive. Young birds still wear
their mottled brown; adults gleam shiny black.
Their whirring feathers, thousands of quick
stubby triangles, strike cool, crisp air
eyeblink fast. They're a living sheet, black lace
spread. These morning minions, too — singly
and all briefly, black sparks of fire — witness.

Dove Hunting, Corporation Style

After the Jeep dumped him off (Ramon's voice,
"Thees good plays; muy birds!") and disappeared,
he'd got himself near the water, armpit
deep in dry horseweeds the wind scraped through.
Behind him the cottonwoods fluttered pink-
gold across the tank. His gun breathed Hoppe's;
he stuffed it full of crisp blue shells, snicked
the safety on, lit a cigarette, watched
the breeze waver his smoke, saw far-off dots, doves
racing with a tailwind.

                 Two thousand miles
away dreamed his empty desk and yesterday's
sheaf of plans and schedules. Over thirty years
since he'd hunted. Pointing gray wings, a pair
of doves banked just above him; he swung the Browning up,
thumbed the button, and just as they cocked their wings,
slammed the lead bird (folded it over), shucked
the empty, pointed ahead of blurring wings,
jolted his shoulder. Returner's luck: they bounced
once ten feet apart near feather-flecked water.

The swift gray-winged jet that had dropped his group
had sucked its curved door up, whirred slowly
to the end of the long gray strip, made a roaring run
at the far hills, swooped up into the clouds.
Small talk in the limousine, cerveza
and tacos for lunch at the club, dusty
Jeep to sudden isolation reward
of afternoon waterhole, gray sky with wind
lapping gilded leaves, speeding dots: las palomas.

Problem in Translation

Looking for mushrooms, we find a great buck,
his grace slowly turning into a stench
almost visible, a hovering dark
smoke column of flies; seething slowly
in thin gravy, the tossed rice of a thousand
weddings quivers, maggoting about
still bones. My last son whispers, "It's awful."

Months later he holds the skull's ten-point rack,
asks, "Where'll we put it?" His nose is pinched
although the bleaching has left the bones starkly
clean, pure as stone.

     "How 'bout the barn, so
we can see it?"

    "It won't look right." His brow
wrinkles; he points to a bare oak: "Out
there on that tree will do. Use nails; be careful."

Sunday Crappies

Mom said I was old enough to decide:
I chose the fish in Murray's Lake. Next dawn
Tom and I threw long-shanked hooks dripping chicken
guts into dark smoking water, hauled in
a pair of gun-blue-sided, fork-tailed cats.
My Mass was the sun that lit lily stalks
musing deep blue water. A great hawk
screamed, smacked down, labored up clutching a fish.

The bridge's all-night fisherman watched
his goosequill float slide, vanish. Spray-taut line,
dancing bamboo C: gauze-finned crappie,
first I'd seen. He held it up, pinched its gills,
unhooked it, tossed it behind him to flop.
He lay down his pole, pulled up his stringer;
my eyes bulged. "God, Tom! Look at that." We sighed:
at least forty fish. Dripping charred headlines,
they lay flashing silver. He attached his catch,
lowered them again, rebaited, threw out.

Sometimes since, a shaft of light at Mass
loosens memories of the Marais des Cygnes
bottom, my guilty pleasure, the diving hawk,
a dripping stringer of night-caught crappies.

Fall Murrain

Across the valley my son had mowed in June,
far trees turned yellow and bronze await
further magic touches. A mere hundred
yards downhill thirty-five wild turkeys form
a skirmish line and glean through ironweed
for grasshoppers. I crouch behind buckbrush,
fill my eyes with their shining, dark-
feathered bodies. They cluck to each other,
carefully pick their ways, rustling thin cover.
When my dog sees them, he bounds past me.
Their heads swivel instantly up at his bark;
they crouch, spring, great gray-white barred wings thrash
free air, and the little valley is alive
with their passage. They scatter into the weeds
of the hill over east. Soon I hear
them calling each other, watch them unfreeze
from where they've hidden, file furtively up
the slope and disappear beneath far trees.

Warm sunlight fills my valley, tempers the breeze;
migrating monarchs straggle slowly south.
A Chicago-bound jet, so high it's just
a dot, sails oblivious of us lowly
beings: scattered seeds, fowls, insects, me.
More and more I feel the pull to shed my skin,
unfurl damp iridescent wings, fly south.

Square Yard

I found his patch of ground, roughly square,
scraped free of grass and leaves to bare dirt.
I looked at it in the twilight; his sharp
hooves had left herringbone scratches deep
in the clay, center dark with his scent.
Some deer had bounded away, brown hair
blending with the brush, flagtail curt,
as I came. Bare trees stirred, a wind harp
quietly sighing soft things of sleep.
Standing there so still as the light went,
I felt at home, another black tree
stripped by wind, my rifle a stone limb
pinned to bent arms. I pulled hard to swim
free, climb the hill, find fires lit for me.

Great Jays

A blue-gray flash under the trees caught
my eye: a great hawk darted down,
struck a busy barred-rock hen, exploded
a flurry of wings, threshing
in fallen leaves; briefly it looked
as if the chicken would break free; it could
not escape sharp talons, a huge black
beak, hatcheting again and again.

I called my son; as we crept near,
the falcon raised up, struggled to carry
away its kill, left it, and sped off,
swooped up into an oak. Later
it dropped back, pinned down its prey,
tore ragged beakfuls of feathers, ate.
My son's hunting eyes grew wide as he watched
the noisy flaying, the hawk dipping
to its bloody meal, its raptor vigilance.
Full, the bird leaped, banked, vanished,
a living dart under the trees.
"He's like a great jay," said my son.

Loner

Just before our truck, slowing for the turn,
jolts in the ruts, I see my son bending
in Scott's field; he straightens up, sends
us a glance, and bows again to the burned-
red-by-drought wild strawberries. We stop, ask
if he wants a ride; he waves us on.
The dust billows behind us, is soon gone
in the trees. Tired by a long day, I bask
in the joy of seeing him: so what
if alone? His dog chases rabbits, the larks
lace the sky with song, he knows the flowers.
Not long, now, before our thinning ties are cut;
he's surveying his own lights and darks.
I wish him peace in these questing hours.

Fish Story

My father described his ice shanty, how once
against the circle of broken crockery
he'd scattered by handfuls trickling down
for background, there'd come — oh of course as
quick
as thought and silently — the sudden
presence — he'd spread his arms wide — a great
sharp
darkness to nose at the lure dangling —
how he'd had to look twice to believe . . .
In that cold dim hut with its spear out
the top as pupil/beam of the eye of light —
the shack subtly lit by diffusion,
soft light through the sullen ice itself —
his hands had sweated on that cold shaft
of hickory from his father's grove and knife —
he'd double-checked that the grains were across,
then thrust down with all his strength, the jolt
straining his shoulders, the racketing silent
explosion, the tugging line. The taut
jerking cord wet his hands as he pulled;
the fish came up, plates bending, a drift
of blood like smoke.

Watching Blues

A cold-in-the-shadow day, wind burning
fingers red, and a gun-gray sky —
cutting or hauling wood, digging
the last carrots or potatoes
out of the frost-flattened garden —
I hear them sometimes, faintly,
like far off terriers brushpiling
a rabbit; I straighten up,
glad to rest, and look for a dark
smudge, ragged files, or perfect vee.
I watch them out of sight, haunted
by their flimsy strength.

"I'll be home soon, Mom," I'd call, looking
back over my double-barrel, her standing,
watching me go. "Take care," she'd say.
I took time to get way downwind and drop
into a gulley. I crawled carefully through
black ooze, keeping the muzzle free, cradling
the twelve gauge above my mucky elbows.
Wisps of wheat shielding me, I poked up
my head to feast: they fed, scattered
like crumpled newspapers on the wheat.
Alarmed, frantic wingbeats, the air filled
with beating kites, they clawed the wind.
Touching with my eyes was enough.

My older brother jabs his finger southwest,
"See, there they are!" I squint into the sun;
I see feathery cirrus against washed sky.
"Just keep lookin'," he says, "you'll see 'em."
I bore holes in the clouds with my eyes.
Way off they turn as one — the sun slants off

their wings — dust motes in a dark room
in a beam of light, becoming invisible
as they fly downwind. Like a minnow shoal
they swim off into the deep water sky.

Hands sticky black from digging sweet potatoes,
I hear their calls like distant cries for help
and look helplessly at their tattered line.
I call to my son: he leaves his wagon and runs
to stand with me, squinting after them. I tell
him about flying over Swan Lake, the thousand-
wing cloud, how a goose looks back at the plane,
wings over and plummets down. I stand close
to my father in an old sun and watch
a thin line blur off into the clouds.

Three Evenings, Three Apples

I

On the evening of Martin Luther King's
Day I crept down from my garage roofpeak
to the eave; my aluminum ladder propped
there would let me climb to frozen ground.
I had cleaned my smoking flue with a chain
on a rope, replaced the now-cool cap, tossed
the cleaner to the sidewalk below. Poised
correctly for a split second on the rungs,
I thought that, should it slip, I'd grab the trough.
The ladder's feet scooted — I fell backward,
almost instantly bouncing on my back
atop my quivering ladder. My head roared
with rosy light — pain had color, then — I rolled
over on all fours and cried out feebly
to frozen earth, then crawled into my garage
and scratched the kitchen door. The shock
of striking — and just the numbing impact of
a sudden nine-foot drop — had begun to wear
away when they found me.

                         A slow week
later, shifting my aching foot, I knew
my good luck that the only bone to break
fills my left big toe. It was late and *Nightline*
showed the seven astronauts crawling
out of their high cabin. Minor mishaps had
delayed their great leap, an orbiting, first
step to the stars. My foot and envy hurt.

II

A huge crowd had collected beneath a sky
so blue it rivaled heaven's own. High
and far, it seemed to beckon them all,
especially the chosen seven. Tall
with joy and pride each took his special place —
just before, a helper with smiling face
gave the teacher an apple — to wait
through another countdown and achieve the great
step to space. Waiting people prayed and hoped
for a successful launch, the great rope
of fire and smoke leading aloft, a sign
of grace and force wedded to right design.
The gantry with its proud rockets and craft
loomed beyond the carnival scene; the throng laughed
and cheered as checktests were passed. The controlled
fury: jets blasted power, smoke billowed, rolled.
Majestically the mighty venture rose
to an instant when everything froze.
It was that moment, height and speed both gained,
to blast free of thick air and win free again.
As if the very sun had blinked and gone out —
all the excited laughter and glad shouts
drained from exultant, triumphant faces —
a great clap in the air! The rocket's traces
slowly arced down, down to splatter and splash
a calm blue sea with bits of useless trash.
A dream — no, millions of dreams — shattered
in a mere bulging flash. But all that mattered,
mattered still. In counting it up, the cost
seems clearer. These fine, precious lives we lost
are only another payment we've made
and the end is out of sight in the shade
of the stars in our eyes and hearts. We thirst,
unslaked; we must voyage and find out the worst,

if in all this speckled darkness no lover,
demon or other, may be. Discover
it we will, or like these beloved seven
be translated in a flash into heaven.

III

Munching on my saved-from-lunchtime
apple, I leave my desk, descend
hollow stairs to push my way
through glass doors, limp slowly
to the parking lot and find
my old truck. The sky is filmed
with lacy cirrus and the sun
centers a rainbow. A side glance
at its brilliance recalls
the sudden burst of light
at their going
and I choke on my apple,
then swallow hard, walk on.

Hunter

It matters to me that the field below
the north creek looks like a great piece of whole
wheat bread that the knife of morning has sliced
open; the tall ragweeds, silvered with frost,
are the color of deer hair. The sun
on this November Sunday is almost up,
and as I watch, bare branches and trunks
turn rose. I follow my rifle-crossed shadow
up the hill and over, stop to view Bear
Creek valley at dawn. Far off, guns fire
and crows call; below the hill a turkey's
"Tock, tock, tock" signals feeding. The first
whitetail's alarmed bounds vanish in oak leaves.
I stand long and still against an oak trunk,
wait for a feeding button buck to clear
a screen of hazel and wild plum. My shot
drops him to a bed of crimsoning leaves.
His entrails smoke as they spill into cold air;
I cut a stick and wedge open his ribcage,
begin the long drag through brambled woods.
Unseen, a circling redtail soars and screams.

Mounting the steps, we enter a filled church
and see the congregation's coat of many
colors; the people look like banks of flowers.
The priest and servers sweep up the aisle
to lighted candles and organ swells.
Beginning the ritual, he welcomes us
and speaks of sacrifice, linking bread and fire,
blood and hope, the enigma that is Christ.
While the priest prepares our gifts, part of me
relives my solemn sacrifice of joy.

When he holds up the wafered bread, I see
the eaten moon over my shoulder. The wine
quivers in it golden cup — its redness
fires fallen leaves, smokes warmly in the sun.
Never ever worthy, I must sound my bell,
cry out "Unclean!" always, not discuss it.
I offer my field of bread and the clear
morning, the fat flesh of my little buck,
she who warms my back, our children, our breath.
Shuddering, I eat the broken bread, sip
the blood, and swallow my faith in nothing.

Working

The Use of Concrete

We tack the boards up, making a box
for the concrete to fill, taking care
to put the smooth side in, hugging the rocks
at both ends, keeping it plumb and square;
finally we're ready — the steel all tied
down the center, braces on hand or nailed
in place; we wait for the truck outside
and talk over old jobs, forms that have failed
and ruined the work; we guide him in close,
snap down the spout and carefully pour
the slurry, tapping the boards so it flows —
screeding, floating, troweling is how it grows
into the lasting dilemma of form
like a magic womb: divinely gross.

Fall Turning

Standing in frost-silvered stubble,
I hold my rifle, call him;
he grunts up. I point between
his eyes, an inch up, half an inch
to the left.

                    As he falls,
Uncle's knife blinks beneath
the jowl. "Dummkopf!" cries my tiny
aunt, darting her cup to catch red
spurting, "die Blutwurst." I help
tie the rope; hemp tearing at
my fingers, we drag it under the maple
where we swung giddy last summer.

                    Flame
tongues lick the barrel; we scald and scrape,
wash clean; I watch tumbled coils
spill smoking into air, saw grate
down silver spine.

                    We strain for bristle
on a window screen, turn the guts inside
out over the garden, scrape
and wash them: sausage casings.

                    Later
I stop at the feed door,
remember.

View from the Lot

I look up from my fencefixing around
the barn and lot, see my wandering sons
exploring the far grove, the creek that loops
across our pasture.

           Standing there, I see
through my remembering eyes my father
pausing at his work.

                I drive staples
into ancient hedge, tighten wires and hum
a bit. Oh let fences fail and fall—
I'm pleased beyond words with what goes on.

Escape

You know just how it could happen — a snarl,
menacing teeth filling the big hole
where the limb broke off, the den entry,
squirrel got away in the upper hollow,
fear driving it high up so tight
away from hot breath and growls, teeth
rending his thin tailbone. Even an hour
later, ravenous 'coon gone, the squirrel
stuck there safe from everything. Surely
the time seemed long in the empty dead elm
limb — coffin wood, the English say. Your chain-
saw spews out bits of cured squirrel, gray
worms in granola that your cat comes mewing
to, licks hungrily.

Beast

Carrying fencing tools on my way to fix
the watergap — great coil of wire, barbs arm-
oring my shoulder — I met him at the creek,
so dry only a few pools remained.
He'd crawled up the stony trail on crooked
legs, a spiked ridge of shell guarded his back,
the color of mud. We stopped. He thrust
his triangular snout, big as my fist,
out at me; near-sighted, he peered at me.
He was bigger than a dinner plate.
I smashed his head with my rusty old hammer,
picked him up carefully by his scaly tail,
tossed him into the thistles. Heart pounding,
I walked on to cool trees, my watergap.

Gray Lady

Surely, somehow when I least
expect her, she'll be here. Tomorrow,
say, or years off. I'll look up
into her smiling clear eyes. She'll
bend down from a circle of faces,
or she'll step from the slim trunks
of the hickory grove
on a hillside I'm clearing
with chainsaw and axe. Probably
we won't even speak — her smile
will be enough. I'm certain
I'll know, my heart will lift
and shrug off a weight
I hadn't realized was
crushing me. I'll slough
it all as easily as tulips
give their petals to the wind,
leaves scatter, snow feathers
angle down. Oh, being here's
good. But as if dreaming,
I'll be stirred awake:
practice over, the real
commences. All done with clay,
I'll turn to light.

Respite

Winter slackens its grip one day this mid-
February; I lug my saw to a glade
filled with honeylocusts' iron gray.
Frost still lies in gray fern layers; my breath
hangs a wreath of fog. By mid-morning sun
I've felled a dozen trees, left scattered piles
of cream-and-chestnut chips, worked up a sweat.
I set down my noisy smoking saw, rest
on trimmed logs. The hum of bee wings fills this
place.
They've come by thousands from their wintry hives
to sip sweet locust sap, to crawl, tumble
in scented dust. Resuming my work, I'm wary
lest they sting me. But busily drinking
in the spring, they're drunk, tipsy as me.
Although inebriate, I go slow
with my chainsaw: sober, steady, deadly.

Cold Time

I left the conference full of smoke
and wordy frustration, soothed
myself with monotonous long drive home:
rhythms of wipers, sizzling
tires, gray-veiled rain helped me dream
through slow hours of misty dark.

After hellos they said frozen calf.
Vet had come. Heat lamps, straw,
calf making it.

His quick panting, hoarse rasping,
filed my ears.
Three drugstore days later,
back to the cow.

But his hind feet ballooned,
gangrened, rotted off.

I talked it over with my wife,
my son, my neighbor,
my vet; I looked long at the calf,
took my hammer for a dawn
treatment, stroked him down,
ripped his carotid
with my pocketknife.

I dragged him off to the brush,
blackbird food by the creek;
I prayed going and coming,
coming and going.

Morning Coffee

The eyes of men in the coffee shop light up
and follow, through steam and cigarette haze,
every movement of Lola, honey-blonde
(perhaps a bit unnatural shade
heightening what was rather mousy brown),
as her tight jump-suited form fills our cups;
her arm stretches, smooth and round; a breast grazes
a shoulder; hot coffee gushes. A fond
thought like a common dream — a vision played
out like a horizontal dance — surrounds
us. Singly or by pairs we leave to shop,
desk, waiting truck; we're warm with coffeed heat
against the winter; spring waits our next stop
here with summer cups and forbidden sweets.

Hawk's Wheel

I trudge my fence-fixing rounds
and look up at sky-embracing reveling
hawks riding the spring wind
between dappled sky and field.

Motley blackened posts, crooked hedge,
hold up rusted wire. I pound new
staples in, restretch and patch the strands,
straighten or replace old posts with steel.

Skunk cabbage clumps and mustard blooms
divert me; I bend to wild strawberries' white,
admire the buds of saplings creeping
in from the timber, wanting back the pasture.

Having run the edges, I take down the gap,
pull it aside; they'll find it open soon enough.

Poem as Waterline

My torch whooshes its blue flames against
bright-burnished copper. Sputtering flux
dazzles away, blackens; hot solder sucks
back into the joint, drips down on my tensed
leg. I set down the roll, cold rag turns steam:
waterline complete. The torch pops black
and I turn on the valve, hoping no crack
silvers dark spaces beneath the beams.

Fluxmakers' labels all agree, no need
even to wipe clean, yet I scrape and ream
each fitting, cutting them just so, keeping track
of pipe tension, unhurried the best speed.
I've learned it does no good to curse and scream
so I solder right if I want it to take.

Open House

With his rusty key the water man
probes deep under the grass, turns a valve
by feel. I thank him, open the kitchen tap,
let water trickle out; dark red bits
of rust and sediment mark a gritty
channel through the sink's dust. My eyes sweep
faded wallpaper, chipped paint, rippled floor;
cobwebs and light brown dust film everything.
A dead wasp lies near an empty soap dish.
Through years of rainspots I see willow leaves,
yellow spears with crimson tips, by the creek.
The tap splatters on, cool now, and clear.
I find an old cheese glass on a shelf, wash it,
splash it full, hold it dripping to the light;
within the blue-green fleur-de-lis, bubbles,
dust motes circle; slowly I slake my thirst.

Crawl Spaces

The torch pours blue flame curling around
bright copper; the flux sizzles, turns black:
my worm of solder melts, disappears,
I wipe the joint with a damp rag, freezing it,
move the flame to another fitting.

"I'll kill you, you dumb Polack bastard!"
Fuzzy stuck his booze-lit face into
the dark crawl space. "Go ahead and bitch,
you stupid turd. At least you can do
that." He flung the tools under the house.
They appalled me. The plumbers wrangled,
cursed, shouted insults, but calmed for a lunch
together: Fuzzy and Boley.

            Weeks
later I heard others laughing about
the plumbers' mock fight. Not just my house:
every job they pushed each other
then headed to the Du Kum In Bar
for laughs and drinks. Big money split them:
Boley moved off to a union job,
Fuzzy stayed with the shop.

            I became
his helper. He looked like an old bald
bear but taught me politely. "Buddy,"
he'd say, "always hang it all before
you light your torch." After Boley died
in a cave-in, Fuzzy lost all hope, knew
it was all over, came to work drunk,
stayed lit, made me do it all, bringing
fittings and tools to me, telling how.

When we'd buried him, we drank his rest:
a tide of Bud at the Du Kum In.

"You bastard, Steve!" I shout at the joists,
"Push that damn' pipe down." It inches, slows,
then three feet jab at me. "Take that, Prick!"
"Get your big mouth in the road, Dummy!"
I yell at him, smile into the dark.

Blue Entropy

Looking down from my roaring tractor,
I see remnants of an explosion.
Along the hard path worn by cows,
blue-white tufts of a jay
quiver in the wind.

                    Near midfield,
the scattered feathers suggest the bird
was carried here to an open safe place.
Maybe a house cat, more likely a fox
or shadowy, quick-darting Cooper.
Sudden lunch, all the meat is gone.
I drive on to collect fireplace wood. The jay
continues, too, fueling something wild
still hungry, something that lives here, has
rights in these fields, so calm, peaceful
this bright December afternoon.

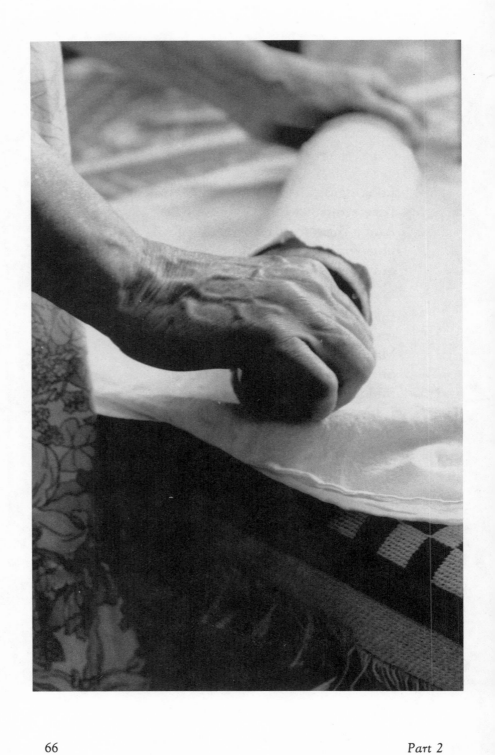

Planter

I stand here, my hands warm
with dishwater, looking
through peach blossoms and shirts
tossing in the sun.

          The wind works
at the window catch, bubbles rainbow
on my busy hands, and all outside
flows drunk with life. I wipe
the glasses and jars quickly
so they won't spot, put the knives
and forks away. The bread mushrooms up,
pale pillows; I butter them smooth
with my fingers, ease them into the oven,
wipe my hands dry, and begin sewing.

The wind flags the shirts; they billow and flap,
kiting and filling out; I listen
to the singing oaks, and sew.

Moon Light

Fetching chopped corn
for the cow, I pour its flurry
into her tongue-polished pan;
my last son buzzes
his imaginary truck
scattering roost-bound hens
and peafowl.

Later he comes inside
where cats lap foam
and groom their whiskers.
The moonlight stripes
floor, flanks, walls,
striping us all
with cool fire.

Leaving the warm strangeness
to the animals,
we bear our pail
of moonmilk home.

Program

Your whisper-touch fingers press
word-processor keys, your blonde
hair wisps against chartreuse
line displays. Then you were working
and I thought of play,
your spider lightness, how
tangled I got becalmed
in the webs of you. Removing a floppy
disc, you'd turn, smile brightly
or wan, go coolly on.

My machine cowers under
its cover of, slight burden of,
dust, and I've gone back to slow
way, to ballpoints and even
lead pencils. I know nibs
and inkwells, quills. Let the machine
wait, dusty and cold, silent.
Your perfume, voice, ragged jeans;
call up any of my programs
and touch me to life again.

Lines for a Good Horse

Announced by our dog's wild barking, the vet
parked his clay-spattered truck, fetched shiny tools,
stood by me as I held my little Arab
horse. I lied to the colt, soothing him, "Relax,
it's okay." His sharp ears perked forward,
he sniffed loudly at the vet's hands, took
pinprick shots — no more than flybites. I led
him about the corral until he wavered,
sank on his side in the dust. I grasped
the lariat looped about his neck, stretched
his hindleg. The vet washed him, splashed iodine:
a flash of scalpel, snipping scissors, two
pink grapefruit segments flung to the weeds.
My horse shuddered once, settled back. The sun
beat down on us; black flies circled, buzzing.
"Make sure he gets plenty of water
and exercise." I wrote out a check, waved
goodbye; minutes later the horse tottered
awake, began to munch thin wisps of brome.

I look at him now, lessened, think briefly
how he might have been a Dan Patch, had I
believed enough, not simply followed logic.
Warmed by our copper sun, a dry wind sighs
about us, stirs the sand of this desert place.

Local Holy Man

Back in those days when priests talked to God
in Latin, Tom Porter filled up the pew
two rows in front of us and two rows
and a space from the celebrant. Tom said
Mass with the priest, gestures and all...eerie
to young, big-eyed me. My mother explained: "They
needed him at home from the seminary.
But part of him stayed; he's never been right since."

Tom worked as a day laborer, made fair
wages, lived quietly, simply, and alone.
Years of walking to and from his field work
left a powerful, gaunt man, grizzled,
yet handsome as a rain-silvered board.
Home from college, I saw him in church, still
saying Mass, still lonely as a jogger,
still accepted as one of us: ours.

My teacher friend Ed told me of being
by chance behind Tom in the supermarket.
"Jim," he chuckled, "he'd stop, look over the grapes,
bless the ones he liked" — Ed signed the cross —
"and eat them. He made a meal of fruit,
crackers, and milk." When I asked Chris, the owner,
hinted at payment, he laughed, "Hell, Jim,
forget it; it's just Old Tom. Have a beer."

One February a blizzard swept in
during early afternoon. "He wouldn't stay,"
Grainger told the sheriff, "nor wouldn't hear
of me taking him home in my four-wheeler.
'It's just a long mile,' he said." He'd slept safely
in a ditch by the highway. Those who saw
him there said afterwards he looked peaceful.

All of us gathered in our Sunday clothes,
talked with God as best we could, and listened
to our priest. This stuck: "Perhaps you've wondered
at how I felt, knowing Tom said the Mass
with me." He paused. "It finally dawned on me
just to be glad I could — and had help. Tom
was a good man; thus, holy. Let us pray."
It looked empty, empty two rows in front.

Night Work

Turning beneath the angled spots
like a dazzling butterfly
struggling in a spiderweb,
the girl singer of the rock
band "Legend" smacks
a sequined tambourine
and struts behind a thin mikestand
as she belts out, mood dances,
"All Through the Night."

Waitresses work the scattered crowd;
beads of sweat pick up light,
slide like pearls from the drummer's face.
Cigarette-smoke veils drift
through blazing floods; listeners,
rapt by her Mooged voice
and urgent hips, suck
their smokes, sip their drinks.
She bows, begins the first set's next
number, sighs into a slow song.

To her, wrapped tightly in light
and sound, halfblinded with glare, pulled
on by the beat, our shapes loom
indistinctly, dark bulges at tables.
Our smoke roughens her throat,
catches at her lungs; our whistling applause
almost startles; she must at times feel
as if her soul is a buffet cheese
nibbled nightly by gray-blurred mice.

The Honey Man

He answered my knock on his kitchen screen door
by sticking his head out of that sweet-smelling
gloom. "What? Yeah, I can let you have a hive."
He led me away from his super-stacked
porch under dark maples to his shop
and showed me the tools he used to build
his hives. Great stacks of them rose to ceiling
joists. "Got over a hundred swarms scattered
around, some almost in Iowa.
A dozen or so of them around Unionville
were fillin' their fifth supers when that damn'
tornado wiped them out. All told, I lost
thirty-five swarms. Me and George went bee-buyin'
to Georgia. Need any honey?"

                                 I carried
my new hive back to his hot kitchen. Glass
containers, all sizes and shapes, lined
the west wall; cardboard boxes bulging jars
crowded around a big oak table
bristling with bottles and jugs. Full quarts
marched along the counter, dusty empties
mounded the sink. A honey extractor
stood next to a high stack of waiting supers.
"How 'bout a gallon of that?" He pointed
to a jug that looked little-girl blonde.
"Bird's foot trefoil, sweet as a first kiss."
I paid, thanked him, took my hive and honey home;
I whistled all the way to my car.

Family

Work Lessons

Bert and his wife moved back, bought Dhu Bell's farm
with the two silos, unused, out behind
the weathered barns. They worked a garden, raised
most of their food. He ran a few cattle
on their hill, kept a team. I helped Saturdays:
shucking corn (how delicious pine-tarred palms
smell!); cutting wood with a cross-cut (Piss
on the saw, Boy; that'll unbind it.);
mucking out the sheds (acrid fresh manure
steaming in the cold). He'd known my grandpa
whom I didn't remember. (You got the same
wild blue eyes, Boy. That Jim — a charming rascal.)
At noon we followed the team in, ate good soup,
a savory lunch Mary liked fixing.
Some cold afternoons we moved shocks, shadows
sliding longer until finally he'd say,
"Knock off, Boy; can't do it all one day."
He'd pay me, we'd say goodbyes, I'd walk home.

On my time I hunted squirrels and rabbits
on his place, knocked pigeons out of the sky
behind his barn, got Dad's cows in at night.

Bert died while I was in Korea; she'd
moved away when I got back. All the sheds,
barns, silos are gone; the smooth brown hills remain.

On Watches

My self-winding watch stopped,
and realizing finally it had died,
I borrowed my son's Eterna
that had belonged to his grandfather
who no longer checked its creeping hands
or anything else, being dead.

I bought it in Korea, in a Quonset
under flowering chestnut trees
whose leaves ruffled up like petticoats in the wind;
I saw it encased, perfect on green velvet,
a simple gold circle; I wound it up,
heard its tick: quietly working, like my father.

Now it circles my wrist, its hands
some kind of gyroscope; images hawk
my inner sky as I write these arcs;
Cygnus, the great cross swan, wheels
its geometry problem about the pole,
reminding me how late the time.

Falcon with Kingbird

It shot low through thick bordering trees,
crossed the road ahead; it was pursued
by a darting kingbird. The blue falcon —
nearly black against overcast sky — swerved,
flapped its wings and dove, trying to escape.
We'd only time to see it fly down
west, a ravine; we drove the curve, quite pleased
to have seen, picked up and continued
our own pursuits, the stasis from our balcony
to the hospital and school where we work.
Recent rains have re-greened our landscape;
no doubt August's sun will burn it brown.
Springs, rivers, the very stars keep flowing
even without an eye to note their going.

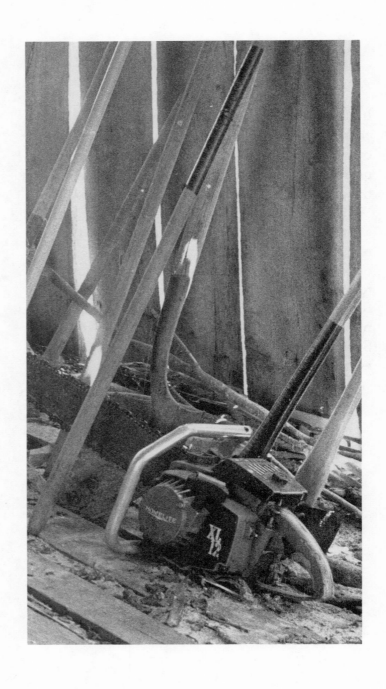

Let the Perpetual Laugh Sound

Happy voices and quiet laughter
from the kitchen awakened
me in my Saturday night bed.
My parents discussed Herman's dream,
a perpetual motion machine,
and Dad's efforts to help craft it;
I drifted back to sleep.

Next week I drank in the hiss
of solder, watched the green flames
of the iron heating, the roaring
blow torch, silver tears of solder,
watched Dad shape the wire rings,
hook them together as a base.

It didn't work. Dad hung the thing
on a nail in the washhouse
and mud daubers, perspicacious ones,
built castles there. But my parent's tones
lilting in my head, dreaming, laugh along.

Caress

A great jagged spark from cloud
to earth, piercing the veil,
then the few second pause before the trail
sound hisses, swishes and window-rattling loud,
tells you what it was you saw.
With luck I once saw the spark
kiss the topmost leaf of wet bois d'arc
and — fiery ball exploding — strip it. In awe
I stepped back from dripping pane
thinking I'd seen the hand
of God. The withered stump remained.
No less amazed years later, I drained
a cup — our eyes met. Then, as if planned,
the whisper of a kiss and thunder again.

Salt in the Beer

At dusk I walk into Vohs' Bar in Wea
to get her a Coke. I recognize some
faces, have the cold can in my hand,
am turning to go: I see him. He waves
me over; we shake hands. In short sleeves,
enjoying a cigarette with his beer,
he sits there. We small talk work, the weather;
before he releases my hand, he scratches
my palm with his index finger and smiles
lopsidedly through the smoke. He knows more
about me — my whispered words over years —
than does any other human being.
This summer Saturday evening
he smirks and scratches my palm. I smile
goodbye.
It is darker outside. I crawl
into the car, hand her the Coke. He's shown
me again what I am. God forgives
but *he* remembers. "See anyone?"
I said 'Hi' to Father. He wished me well."

Desert, Oasis

Going into the desert for a weekend,
I trudged miles of dusty trails just to reach
rocky hills sprinkled with prickly pear, cholla,
saw road runners and huge coveys of Gambrel's,
stepped warily around a sunning snake,
once thought a dark place a tarantula.
Despite thirst, aching muscles, I found peace.
The great sun wheeled above me quicker than
hawks
and eagles. Shadows stretched out from the hill,
lovelier than any cathedral's
High Mass consecration with trembling chords.

Going into her various softnesses,
I swam into breeze-touched petal waves;
feather-light they take the floundering swimmer,
then lift him effortlessly up and down,
floating. And always there's the sense of being
somehow freer as if involved in
music, for once being the song, jungle
drums and damp perfumes. There is no time.
Away from her for long the compass
lies, the arrow flickers back, turns me,
a bonedry dove or hawk, to her oasis.

Washing in Air

Shunted to the back seat by my third son,
I relax in the car and try to sleep.
On the freeway around Kansas City
I see a child's arm extend from the car
speeding next lane to ours; his hand grasps
the air tentatively, releases it, feels
it again. His hand gestures charm me
forty-five years and thirty miles: I reach
out from the back window of our Model A;
shaded by a hedgerow, the air hangs cool
and thick with summer evening. It tugs
at my fingers, presses and nudges my skin.
My small hands are grubby, black-lined with
Uncle John's hayloft. I wash my left hand
in the vanished flow of an old moment.

Miles later under the smooth cloud wedge
and rain veil of a thunderhead, we top
a hill, the asphalt black with wetness, rain
drumming our beetle roof. A half mile
ahead lightning blazes a jagged strobe, lights
up a metal bridge railing, rolls a red
ball spark into the ditch. Wide awake
I'm amazed by even my own heartbeats.

Cissy's *Ciseaux*

Cissy, not my sister,
kept her silver scissors in a round
wicker basket she
called her mending box.
It was deep-brown — dyed raffia —
and also held needles,
yarns and spools of thread, buttons
that rattled a little tin
French hard candy had come
in, and thimbles. Her aunt
had given her the antique one,
slightly battered, of silver-
plated brass. She clipped my bristling
eyebrows and furry ear holes
with her shining scissors.

Long afterwards in French
class when mon professeur
said, "Les ciseaux," and snipped
his forefinger against the second,
I saw Cissy:
long smooth, nylon-clad
legs, warm and round, and her deep-
brown somewhat silky mending
basket — oh, box, then — with just
a few loose threads, felt her dimpled
magic thimble's
tremors. Over and over
I thought, "Les ciseaux,
la Cissy. Les
ciseaux, ma Cissy."

A Breath of Cloves

Garlic clumps flourish by the garden fence;
I kneel to pick some, have to pry out clods
of sunbaked earth for bulbs shaped like pullet eggs.
The plants are gray-green like slender onions
with drouth-browned stalks. They seed themselves
back;
their white bloom turns into tiny sets.

Cleaning the garlic, I remember cold roasts
my dad often sent to me. He froze
them, wrapped them carefully in the *Star*,
shipped them through the mail. My knife parted ice
crystals as I sliced boned meat and garlic bits
he'd flavored the beef with to make my sandwich.

I tear off the outer layers of the bulbs —
old tissue paper with crumbs of dirt,
a knot of walrus-whisker roots. The cloves
cluster round a central stalk. Each segment,
shaped like a miniature orange
slice, plumply fills its delicate pink shell.

Old wives' tales say that garlic deters evil:
the eye and vampires; *Allium sativum*'s
strong smell and spear shape confound
malice. It's taken me long to understand,
but I realize now your gifts, your food:
my heart is yours, vanished vampire father.

Dues

She snapped at the striped kitten,
caught my son's left arm, ripped
the meaty covering by his elbow.

Jealous Sheba, exiled from town
because of her biting incivility.
Now she ran heavily, carrying
pieces of lead in her mouth,
ear and side. She lurched
into the gate, shuddered,
coughed and swayed down.

Dazed by the brain shot, she'd
staggered; she shook her head
as if flies nipped her ear;
the shot into her shoulder
put her down; she limped slowly
to the house, whimpered.

I dragged the sledge near
her fogging eye, swung
a blind arc, blotted her howl.
I took hold of her shivering
foot, dragged her away
from questions into the darkness
below the hill.

Family Quarrel

The Fishers lived two miles east of town on
the east side of north-south gravel: dusty
yard shaded with elms and cedars, green-trimmed
white house, a knot of outbuildings with a pump,
a barn and a windmill blending into stacks
laced together with crooked lanes.

                                    They had
a daughter and twin sons, huge shy young men.
She married and moved to Kansas City, got
a job; her husband drank, they fought, she
came home crying.

                        One dark dawn the husband
came hunting her. With his whispering hand
he quieted the dog; carefully he
sawed a gaping hole in the outhouse door,
sat there rotting in the dark, waiting
for light, stiffened awake at screen door's slam,
and spilled Mr. Fisher on the concrete walk.
He poked his shotgun into the kitchen
and finished breakfast for Mrs. Fisher.
He called his wife's name once up the stairs; she
came slowly half way down with grudging steps,
tumbled on down in an echoing roar;
the twins leaped out of their window, fled
to safety with their neighbors.

                                The sheriff
found them all, including the husband,
quietly at breakfast with the flies.

Hay Crop

Just last year, gnarled as a hedge root,
Bill went sun to sun all summer long, worked
three hundred acres and eighty cows.
He and Mary liked lots of things and being
busy; their kids, grown up, were just the same.
Sometimes the old ones talked about cutting
down, taking it easy, but they didn't.

                        The sun
that ordinary July day had crisped the hay
new-mown by ten to ready by one.
Bill felt the burning metal seat, shifted
his body, and drove out to the baler
waiting in the barn. He hooked it up, dragged
it out to the field, a great saucer spilling
windrows of red clover southwest. On the first round
down in a slough, the baler clogged; Bill stood
straining to clear it when dazzling glory
pinned him on his elbows to the hot steel;
he trembled there in that perfumed oven
until his knees gave way and he dropped flat
to the clipped stems where Mary found him, pulse
draining, struck dumb by the sun, a half hour
later.

He sits under the maples now
and cries, not because he hurts or is mad
but because it ended and didn't.

Stout as an Oak

They're busying themselves with a fort
and raising walls of leaf-and-grass-mottled snow.
I guide my old red tractor through the drifts
and beneath the hill. My reluctance stems
partly from fears. The dead white oak I'll cut
measures a yard and rises from a steep
snow-covered bank. I click the tractor's switch
from roar to loud silence, service my saw,
study the tree.

           Yellowish dust and chips spew
onto the snow; acrid smoke makes me cough.
First cut done, I make the second kerf
angle down, then stop. I tramp smooth a path,
my getaway, rest. Final cut: the blurring
chain buries itself. The great tree mass shifts,
closes my first cut. Now only a thin tongue
of wood holds the bole erect. Cautious,
I spring back when the triangle snaps:
slowly the oak leans, then rushes, crashes down.

While I'm resting, I count the rings and find
this acorn sprouted during the Civil War.
Somewhere inside I still shake — it looked young
just last spring. I take my time, saw half a cord
to heap my trailer, slowly crawl on up hill
to the shed. The boys yell and desert their fort.
Laughing, they run to stack a wall of wood.

Windbreak

Kneeling here on my clay hill,
obscure bulge of an old ice river,
I pat loam around root hairs
and dreams. A linestorm grumbles;
its winds buffet me, threaten
to blow away this world.

Forty years ago I helped plant
a new orchard in the rain:
grandsons lugged heavy buckets,
splashed the finger-sized trunks,
gave a good drink along
the scraggly lines of stakes
marking scrawny seedlings.

With axe and saw we hacked out
the easy; we dynamited the gnarled.
I lit the sputtering fuses,
hid beneath my long father's shadow;
the clods rained us dark.

                    The new trees
mushroomed into sweet clouds, heavy
branches straining low with fruit,
circles of perfumed decay
flowered with fall morning cloaks
and yellowjackets drunk with sun.
Long after, a tin-roof drummed
above his coffin lid. He'd hoped
to perfect perpetual
motion. And did.
He thought he'd failed
the Great Depression. His trees
all gone, we plant these thin lines
beneath the dream-dark mountains, thunder.

Dreams, Endings

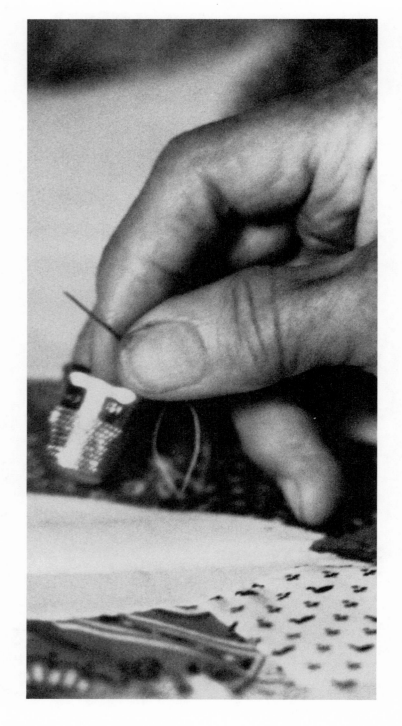

Quilt

I spread it out again, noticing
the dominant pattern of killing
black, the warm juicy reds,
and all those other shades that tend
to trail off into gray, somehow
suggesting a hawk's eye view of fields;

I see the ladies stitching the blocks together,
quilting away, their murmuring
music filling the back porch
or church basement, biting thread
and tying off tufts.

My quilt is new with recent patches
and old with originals; it keeps
me warm, except where the holes are;
if it doesn't look like much to you,
stand off to one side and squint.

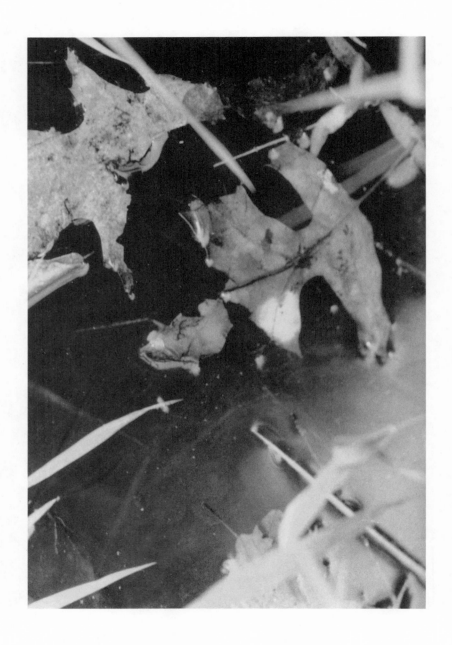

Leaves in Rain

Stepping out into a damp lull
of sidewalks dark from
a fall thunderstorm,
I lean against a wind
driving flocks of harlequin
leaves slanting down northward.
At first they look so like birds
I'm surprised at their misdirection.
Scuffing among their soft
scattered fire, I see they're handfuls
of sun, layers of bright
ash. So I begin to pick
my way more carefully
through their brief coals.

Parachutes

A mixed group of jumpers lounge
under the wing, checking gear,
drinking Cokes and talking.
One, recognizing me as I stride past,
calls out, "Sixteen jumped today!"

After belting in, I sit thinking
back, looking at our slick-skinned wing
angling the mazed horizon,
how my shy father questioned alone
fifty-odd years before jumping.

Off to our left, chutes blossom
like peonies against the clouds.
He'd leapt into the dark
of belief.

Bedtime Story

Once upon a time we sat in a car
in spring beneath a moon that, we knew, would
eclipse around eleven. These few flat
words deal, though poorly, with glory, some strange
occasional mystery — notes in tune
even non-singers rise humming — with heaven
and variant places. We'd turned music on,
something slow-moving, and danced quietly there.
The skin of someone you love picks up sheens and tones
of pearl in moonlight. Parted lips and eyes, gone
now a generation, sparkle still. A strand of hair,
coal black, perfumed: its touch tickles me —
spidery wisp branded me surely
as glowing steel. When I hear an eclipse
discussed, often my mind plunges back
to musky warmth, the blotting out, twice
upon a time or more, heavenly bodies
seemingly motionless in deepest space:
relentlessly forever moving apart.

Enduring a Fall Rain

Millions of the changed leaves, cold-charged reds
and yellows, had fallen; the rest waited, dripped
steadily after two days of slow rain.
Street gutters had been washed clean of drought's
dust yesterday; today's hurrying streams
were little darker than a spring trout brook.
I found myself noting eddies where fish
might wait. Myriad raindrops pattered,
rattled snaredrum tattoos on my taut black
umbrella — the walk was melting ice — each
drop smacked, bounced up a silver nipple;
everywhere was dancing. I splashed along
beneath the thunder; through ribs, thin fabric,
I could see beaded rain. Perhaps up close
death itself might seem as live and soothing.

Some of the Hidden Stars

Rarely does anyone notice, but the leaves
of the sweetgum, *Liquidambar styraciflua,*
a common tree of the South,
look like green stars. Following
the first touch of autumn — the veriest trace —
a few of the leaves become gold.
It's true — with no noise — an ordinary
miracle. Later the green disappears,
replaced by red. On this day
because of the rain the whole world
looks gray; but the leaves shine forth
light as if little suns
lived inside. It's strange:
a leaf dies filled with flame.

Smitty's Bar, LaPlata, Missouri

Mid-March-Saturday-afternoon snow, gray
as dampened ironing — the ragged drifts
barricaded the streets; we'd got the chair
we'd come for carefully loaded and safe
from the splashing slush or spitting sleet.
Debating whether or not to get a drink,
my boys eye the aluminum gray shark,
F-86, posted on concrete supports
in the town park. They talk of dogfights and loops;
empty gun ports ignore our dirt-brown truck,
stare fixedly at the crumbling brick wall
of the old bank opposite. Loaded rigs
whine past the frozen jet's down wheels and flaps.

We stop our truck, cross the street to Smitty's,
and take seats in the booths that line
the north wall. All the stools are full along
the curved bar on the south. The talk drones on
of crops, the hog market, the weather, some-
body's girl — "Some body? Well, Hell yes — tough!"
The bartender brings our pop and beer. We
drink in the blue smoke, flourescent jukebox's
purple vertical stripes snaring silver
circles vibrating with "Dueling Banjos."
Gray light seeps through steamed-over plate glass
windows flanking the front door opening
to admit four ranchers in muddy boots
and curled-brim hats. They call for drinks and josh
their friends at the bar. One takes a long swig
then, after carefully setting down his glass,
does a headstand over the worn oak floor,
scattering cigarettes and matches, but
keeping his hat and smile tightly on.

He picks up his things; his friends roar approval.
An old couple just entering as he leaps
stare; the man says, "Damn fool," and orders beer. My
boys drink their pop. Someone dares the acrobat;
he loops again for a Bud and a burst
of yells; he bows above worn cowboy boots.
A crack — someone has broken the racked
triangle on the pool table as Merle
Haggard whines over the captured guitars. "Dad,
about ready?" He stares, whispers to us,
"The jumper just 'took his finger off.'" Smiling
at the boys, the cowboy repeats it. We
leave as more farmers stream into Smitty's
like birds near dark coming back to water.

We drive slowly past the graven jet, still
poised, cold exhaust and guns empty, landing
forever beneath hovering maples
in the park in LaPlata, Missouri.

Non-Poem

(This is not a poem.
I have put it in free verse form
although it is not free.
It is an essay written for all those
who were not born encauled, nor Plathypusses
ready to drink the belladonna jar empty
in Tennessee, alone on a hill.)

A Nontitle

To the Ordinary Would-Be Poet A Salute

Fellow dabblers of everyday, flies
feebly stirring the tarbaby of self
we're stuck to, cliché mongers all:
What if, when you speak, your words erase sounds
so that the longer you speak, the quieter it gets?
What if, as you speak, the light grows dimmer
and the longer you speak, the darker it gets?
But, fellow would-bes, your hiving hum
produces no change. Nothing registers.
At least, to make nothing would be a sign.

A critic once rightly said my nonpoems didn't sing
and gave me some red-haired music lines
by R. P. Dickey, presumably to inspire me.
I read these again and again; finally
I was glad that he'd left Missouri —
for me, it was non-music.

I feed my cows and calves, my chickens
and ducks, milk, turn out the stock,

and plod back to the house. The fog
fills up the valley — I see it pour
out over the road, spread thinly on the plain;
the sun bursts up, gold fingers on grass,
bathes all in light. The birds
talk to the wind as if a tree has
the soul of a stone.

Estate

Ed and Annie Hartman were my brother's
god-parents, faithfully took up a third
of a pew three rows forward of us, lived
on a farm southeast of town; the house
had a front door with a vertical oval
pane of rim-frosted glass; covered with bluegrass,
the yard got shade from tall red cedars.

We lived several miles away, off north
on the Sheehan place; one branch of Pony Creek
began at our spring. We visited them
several times, knew their rooms' shapes, the bulk
of the upright, dark-varnished piano,
oak tables and chairs, scarf-covered bureaus,
two black stoves, fragile lamps, the screened backporch.

Cars lined both sides of the road a hundred
steps from their mailbox. Knots of people drifted
about the yard; the furniture huddled there
under the trees, was grouped by rooms. No one filled
chairs, rested on a bed. I sipped black coffee,
heard the seller's chant, walked once through hollow
rooms.
Off to the west far bottomland turned blue.

Thirteen Wheels

Mistakenly, we call them locusts here,
loud cicadas that saw light away;
their strident songs fill the oaks I'm under.
I look at some holes the bugs crawled from —
pencil-wide, the ground dark-pocked — as earth
heaves up a few feet away. A mole digs
there, making labyrinths among tree roots.
I watch tremoring grass and dust waver
slowly toward me as if a huge snake
slid ever nearer under the sod.
I freeze on top of throwaway plastic
carapaces and remember my mother's
quick knife into churning garden soil,
worm-like guts of skewered insectivore,
how soft and gray its fur: almost fifty
years ago in the Depression. I wait
quietly to let him pass, let earth look
properly dead and at rest. How strange
to feel kinship with a mole: he is
a tiny, long-digging writer-observer.
What if he gets lost, loses his sense
of direction, vanishes, goes quite blind
probing toward the earth's hot central dark?
He digs near tap roots, rocks, and similar
hard truths. Moles have buried themselves deep
in Amherst, Concord, spied out secrets there.
Cicadas like these will reappear
in thirteen years. I cross my fingers, wish.

Dry Time

At a crowded table in the coffeeshop
eight older men listened to a retiree
with a brown paper sack. "It's full of seeds
from Western Auto," he said. "Now that's gone,
they give 'em to me, so here." He set down
the sack, waved at the men, laughed, "Hell no,
I ain't gonna plant nothing this late, this dry,"
left.

        The man to my right dealt everyone
a packet of seeds, as if they were cards
and this a poker game. I got zucchini.
Across from me, his leathery face earnest,
he talked of evening watering. "It's nice,
sitting in the backyard and listening
to water droplets spattering on corn leaves.
Smells good, too." The dealer looked at his packet,
grunted, "Bloomsdale spinach? That's for spring."
The youngest man there, a grandpa, full beard
grizzling his jaws, was attempting to convince
his neighbor to plant some rattling pumpkin seeds
in his big corn patch. "Hell, the weeds is taller
than the corn, which is curlin'."

                   A pause
followed the screendoor's swing as in walked
an ordinary-long-dark-haired-eyed beauty
wearing a light plaid blouse and snug blue jeans.
As if mesmerized, all the men fell silent;
no heads swung to stare, no one spoke until
she'd bought coffee and a roll and walked out.
"God, it'd be nice to have a little rain."

Toad at Rest

Once upon a day — actually
an evening after chores before all the spring
light had melted away -- Bill and Mary
realized that they had met and fallen
into love and kids and a farm, built
a new house themselves, barns and corral, dug
two ponds and worked a garden, raised cattle,
peafowl, horses and grandkids, enjoyed
more than thirty years of marriage and grown old.

Yesterday's rain keeping him from discing,
Bill picked his way through his garage to drink
his after-supper coffee and smoke
a cigarette on the balcony
and look at the clouds. Mary joined him;
the house wasn't crowded and noisy. "Why?"
said Bill. "Why, generally?" " I don't know,
either," said Mary. "Why bother with canning
beans if there's just you and me to eat them?"

Frogs sang, breeze stirred oak and hickory leaves;
off north a barred owl wondered aloud.
Moths fluttered at the yellow light. "Kiss
me, Prince," she said, "and I'll fix you a second
cup of coffee." "What?" he said. "What? Oh, all
right. Of course; but we toads are pretty
careful. Have to protect the jewels, you know."

They could not hear the clouds' scratching nor faint
clicks of the slowly wheeling galaxy;
they listened to a fan whirring over
the kitchen stove, and the wind's purring.

Credits
Indexes

Credits

All of the photographs in this book have been taken in Adair County, Missouri. One photograph, on page 7, is from the Archives of Pickler Memorial Library of Northeast Missouri State University. The University Photo Journalist, Ray Jagger, took the pictures on pages 2, 4, 8, 13, 16, 19, 22, 44, 50, 74, 78, 86, 92, 98, 100, 104, 106, 116. The author, Jim Thomas, took the photographs found on pages 20, 24, 30, 39, 42, 53, 56, 64, 66, 70, 76, 84, 90, 94, 113. Bob Schnucker is responsible for the pictures on pages 32, 47, 54, 60, and 80.

Index of First Lines

Index of Titles